EDUCATOR COMPANION GUIDE TO THE BOOK

# *Our Stories*

## An Introduction to South Asian America

**Cover image**

Photograph of Eqbal Ahmad teaching students in the late-1960s, likely at Cornell University. In SAADA, courtesy of Julie Diamond.

Edward Said called him "the shrewdest and most original anti-imperialist analyst of Asia and Africa." Born in Bihar in the early 1930s, Eqbal Ahmad lived a life that crisscrossed the globe; he was a journalist, an activist, and in the words of Noam Chomsky, a "counsellor and teacher." He arrived in the U.S. in the '50s as a fellow at Occidental College, later earning a Ph.D. at Princeton. Throughout his life, Ahmad was at the center of key moments in anti-imperialist history. As a young man, he traveled to Algeria, joining the FLN (National Liberation Front) with Frantz Fanon. In the '60s, Ahmad became a powerful voice in opposition to the Vietnam War and U.S. foreign policy in the Middle East. Ahmad, alongside several anti-war Catholic activists, was arrested on charges of conspiracy to kidnap U.S. National Security Advisor Henry Kissinger, a case that ended in a mistrial in 1971. Ahmad would go on to hold several teaching positions in the U.S. at the University of Illinois-Chicago, Cornell, and Hampshire College. When asked by the journalist David Barsamian on what he tells his students, Ahmad responded: "I don't tell them anything. I think that my life and my teachings all point to two morals: think critically and take risks."

Copyright © 2021 by *the South Asians for Educational Justice Collective.*

## Table of Contents

| | |
|---|---|
| 1 | Introduction |
| 4 | Alignment to Common Core Standards |
| 5 | Activity Ideas with Content from Our Stories |
| 5 | *Activity 1: Gallery Walk with Excerpts from the Book* |
| 11 | *Activity 2: South Asian Women Workers* |
| 12 | *Activity 3: Resisting Violence and Xenophobia* |
| 13 | *Activity 4: Organizing for Change* |
| 14 | *Activity 5: Visual Timeline of South Asian American History* |
| 15 | Discussion Prompts for Deep Reading of Our Stories |
| 20 | Overarching Discussion Questions for Further Exploration of Themes in Our Stories |
| 21 | Discussion Questions by Chapter |
| 31 | Handouts on South Asian Americans |
| 31 | *Who Are South Asian Americans?* |
| 32 | *Short Timeline of South Asian Americans in the U.S.* |
| 38 | Glossary of Terms |
| 40 | Further Resources |

# INTRODUCTION

This companion to the book *Our Stories: An Introduction to South Asian America* offers educators suggested discussion questions, activities, and excerpts to explore issues of identity, belonging, collective action, and social change. The book—divided into ten chapters—covers many more themes than that, but our group of educators, who teach at K–12 and higher-education institutions, privileged the themes of identity, intersectionality, agency, and resistance given our commitments to ethnic studies and social justice education. We were particularly interested in the relational components of the South Asian American experience—in other words, how South Asians have developed their identities, forged alliances, and shaped a sense of belonging in the U.S. alongside other communities, particularly other communities of color. We also focused on how larger xenophobic narratives and policies have been resisted and organized against for greater equity and justice.

As the book notes, there are now nearly 5.4 million individuals in the U.S. who trace their heritage to South Asia. Definitions of South Asian Americans vary, but they often include those who hail originally from the nations of Afghanistan, Bangladesh, Bhutan, India, Maldives, Nepal, Pakistan, and Sri Lanka. The community also includes "twice migrants"—members of diasporic communities in the Caribbean (Guyana, Jamaica, Suriname, and Trinidad and Tobago), Africa (Kenya, South Africa, Tanzania, Uganda, and Zanzibar), Canada, Europe, the Middle East, and the Pacific Rim (Fiji, Indonesia, Malaysia, and Singapore) who have subsequently migrated to the United States. South Asian Americans as a group are tremendously diverse, not just in terms of national origin, but also in terms of language, socioeconomic status, immigration status, education, length of time in the country, and where in the country they reside. South Asian Americans may practice one of many religions—the Baha'i Faith, Buddhism, Christianity, Hinduism, Jainism, Judaism, Islam, Sikhism, or Zoroastrianism—or no religion at all.

In this companion guide, we offer prompts and ideas for educators to take into junior high or high school (grades 7–12) or college classrooms, given the topics covered, such as systemic racism and violent forms of discrimination. (This companion could also be utilized by parents to lead discussions with their children at those grade levels, or in after-school or community group settings to guide discussion.) We have created a comprehensive list of guiding questions for each chapter so that educators can assign parts of the book or get ideas of how to link the book's content to other lessons. The companion seeks to offer ways for educators and students to engage with the following essential questions:

1. How do South Asian immigrant communities resist forces of xenophobia, racism, and marginalization in the United States at different historical moments?
2. In what ways do individual agency and collective action shape how South Asian Americans build community and advance their rights in the U.S.?
3. How do South Asian American histories contribute to our larger understanding of U.S. history?

We also provide links to other resources—such as digital timelines, films, and other curricula—to offer educators ideas about how to incorporate South Asian American histories and experiences into their classrooms.

For the past several years, our group has focused on creating accessible resources for educators, based on our collective knowledge as educators and activists. We work with educators in workshops, such as the annual Teachers for Social Justice conference in the Bay Area, to demonstrate how they can examine South Asian American history critically in their classrooms. We hope that this companion guide is useful in your efforts, and we are happy to support you in this work wherever possible, so please feel free to be in touch.

Sincerely,

*The South Asians for Educational Justice Collective*
THE SOUTH ASIANS FOR EDUCATIONAL JUSTICE COLLECTIVE

Monisha Bajaj
*Professor, International & Multicultural Education, University of San Francisco*

Mona Chitkara
*Educator, Peer Resources and San Francisco Unified School District*

Malathi Iyengar
*Associate Professor, Ethnic Studies, College of San Mateo*

Nirali Jani
*Assistant Professor, Education, Holy Names University*

Simmy Makhijani
*Assistant Professor, Asian American Studies, California State University, Northridge*

Gautam Premnath
*English Teacher, Castro Valley High School*

Ruchi Rangnath
*Assistant Professor, Teacher Education, University of San Francisco*

Contact us at saejcollective@gmail.com

## ALIGNMENT TO COMMON CORE STANDARDS

*This Companion Guide is aligned with the following Common Core Standards:*

Reading Standards for Informational Texts

- Integrate and evaluate multiple sources of information presented in different media or formats (e.g., visually, quantitatively) as well as in words in order to address a question or solve a problem.

Reading Standards for Literacy in History/Social Studies (6712)

- Key Ideas and Details
  - Cite specific textual evidence to support analysis of primary and secondary sources, attending to such features as the date and origin of information.
  - Determine the central ideas or information of a primary or secondary source.

- Integration of Knowledge and Ideas
  - Compare and contrast treatments of the same topics in several primary and secondary sources.

# ACTIVITY IDEAS WITH CONTENT FROM OUR STORIES

---

**Activity 1: Gallery Walk with Excerpts from the Book**

GOALS/OBJECTIVES

- *Option 1.* Students will silently read the excerpts, quotes, and facts and/or view images that portray examples of racism and xenophobia against the South Asian American community, as well as those that illustrate resistance and solidarity. Using sticky notes, they will write their thoughts in one word or a phrase to place around the document. These can be reactions, emotions, or connections they have to the material.

- *Option 2.* After reading the documents, students will stand next to one that resonated with or stood out to them to read back to the group.

- *Option 3.* Same as option 1, but students will write down on sticky notes if the text is an example of solidarity, resistance, anti-Black racism, coalition building, agency, or xenophobia.

POSSIBLE DEBRIEF PROMPTS

- What are the most compelling reasons for recovering "hidden" histories (those that don't get told)? Whose stories get told and/or whose stories get hidden?

- What can our community histories show us about resistance in the future?

MATERIALS: Sticky notes, pens.

*To prepare: Each excerpt should be printed on a piece of paper (can be put in sheet protectors).*

Sample Gallery Walk Excerpts

**Kala Bagai**: In 1921, Vaishno naturalized as a U.S. citizen, but tragedy struck the family when he was stripped of his citizenship on the basis of not being white in the wake of the 1923 Supreme Court case of *United States v. Bhagat Singh Thind*. Vaishno was forced to liquidate his property, including his store in San Francisco. Furthermore, he was denied a U.S. passport to visit India and was told he should reapply for British citizenship (which he had renounced to become a U.S. citizen) and try to get a British passport. Increasingly disillusioned, Vaishno rented a room in San Jose and committed suicide by poisoning himself with gas in 1928. (From "Kala Bagai," p. 67)

**Unfair and Lovely**: *Unfair and Lovely*, a response to the widely promoted skin-lightening cream Fair and Lovely, is a 2015 photo series featuring South Asian sisters Mirusha and Yanusha Yogarajah, created by Black American artist Pax Jones to combat "colorism on a global scale by highlighting its intersectionality." In 2016, it sparked an online campaign, in collaboration with *Reclaim the Bindi*, featuring women of color around the world posting photos of themselves with the hashtag #UnfairAndLovely. (From "Unfair and Lovely" inset, p. 174)

**Chandra Gooneratne**: Chandra Dharma Sena Gooneratne left Ceylon (now Sri Lanka) in the 1920s to get his doctorate at the University of Chicago. He began traveling around America giving lectures on a variety of topics, including abolishing the caste system and the movement for independence in India. As a result of his travels, and like other visiting scholars from Asia and Africa at the time, Gooneratne encountered anti-Black racism. But he also began to realize that he could use his turban while traveling in the Jim Crow South to avoid harassment. At times he encouraged others to do the same, writing, "Any Asiatic . . . can evade the whole issue of color in America by winding a few yards of linen around his head. A turban makes anyone an Indian." (From "Chandra Gooneratne" inset, p. 78)

**J. J. Singh and Enuga Reddy**: J.J. Singh, perhaps the most influential South Asian American in the 1930s and 1940s, developed close ties with Walter White, the executive secretary of the NAACP, and the two worked together to defend the rights of South Asian Americans and African Americans and to support the political independence and economic development of India. Another prominent South Asian American, Enuga Reddy, built ties with African Americans while working against South African apartheid as an official at the United Nations. (From "The Civil Rights Movement," pp. 87–88)

**Dalit Panthers**: Formed by a group of writers and poets in 1972 Bombay in reaction to widespread violence against Dalits across India, Dalit Panthers was a liberation movement inspired by the Black Panther Party of the United States. The militant movement organized against the oppressive caste system in India and fought to eradicate the concept of "untouchability" in the country. The group led marches, rallies, and visits to "atrocity" sites to lend support to victims of caste violence. In their manifesto, issued in 1971, the Panthers wrote: "From the Black Panthers, Black Power was established. We claim a close relationship to this struggle." (From "Dalit Panthers" inset, p. 87 and "What Dr. B. R. Ambedkar Wrote to Dr. W. E. B. Du Bois," p. 181)

**Post-1965 Immigration**: The 1965 Immigration Act opened up new immigration opportunities and transformed South Asian America. The law ended discriminatory national-origin quotas that had regulated immigration since the 1920s and established, in its place, a system that privileged families seeking to reunify and "highly skilled" applicants in specific fields. Immigrants with expertise in the sciences and health fields were especially sought after to meet growing demands in these parts of the United States' postindustrial economy. South Asian immigrants started arriving in growing numbers. From 1980 to 2013, the Indian immigrant population doubled every decade, growing from 206,000 to 2.04 million. They now account for 4.7 percent of the foreign-born population. Pakistanis similarly experienced a growth in population. By 1990, there were about 100,000 Pakistani Americans, and there are now more than 409,000 Pakistanis in the country. (From "Post-1965 Immigration," p. 96–99)

**The "Model Minority" Myth**: The "model minority" myth refers to the harmful idea that certain groups are so successful that they are able to transcend their social status as minorities. This cultural expectation is often placed on Asian Americans, including South Asians, and creates a false narrative that all Asians are smart, wealthy, and hardworking—which in turn is used to argue that Asians are less in need of government assistance and are more deserving of praise than other communities of color. The myth creates an incorrect perception that Asians not only primarily have jobs as doctors, lawyers, and engineers, but also are "docile" and nonconfrontational people, thus examples of the "model" way to assimilate into American culture. In popular culture and political discourse, this myth is used as a wedge to separate Asian Americans from others, especially Black Americans. (From "The 'Model Minority' Myth" inset, p. 112)

**Bangladeshi Immigration**: The Diversity Immigrant Visa Program of 1990, also called the Diversity Lottery or the Green Card Lottery, has been pivotal in increasing the number of Bangladeshi immigrants in the United States. Established with the aim of diversifying the country's immigrant population, the act annually sanctions fifty-five thousand permanent-resident visas for natives of countries that have low rates of immigration to the United States. . . . In 2013, however, Bangladesh was deemed ineligible for the Diversity Immigrant Visa Program. While the Green Card Lottery and employer and family sponsorship have served as the main legal mechanisms propelling Bangladeshi migration to the United States, more recent accounts show the presence of a small but growing group of undocumented migrants from Bangladesh. (From "Bangladeshi Immigration," pp. 116–17)

**The Post-9/11 Backlash and Response**: South Asians, Arabs, Muslims, Hindus, and Sikhs endured a double grieving after 9/11, as community members began to experience acts of discrimination, violence, and profiling. . . . Unfortunately the backlash was not limited to the years immediately after 9/11. In 2012, the Sikh Temple of Wisconsin became a site of horrific violence when a white supremacist killed six worshippers on a Sunday morning. In 2015, a young Black Muslim boy by the name of Ahmed Mohamed was placed in juvenile detention after school administrators in Irving, Texas, assumed that a homemade clock Ahmed had made as a science experiment was a bomb. In 2016, South Asian, Arab, and Muslim passengers reported being removed from airplanes because airline personnel or fellow travelers complained that they behaved "suspiciously" by speaking in Arabic on the phone or wearing a hijab and asking to change seats. And in the time since Donald Trump was elected, hate crimes against these groups have continued to grow. (From "The Post-9/11 Backlash and Response," pp. 136–37)

In the wake of 9/11, organizations such as South Asian Americans Leading Together (SAALT), the Sikh Coalition, and Muslim Advocates began taking shape to be leading national voices on issues ranging from discrimination to profiling. At the local level, organizers and advocates at DRUM–South Asian Organizing Center (New York City), Chhaya CDC (New York City), the Arab American Association of New York, the South Asian Network (Los Angeles), the Arab American Action Network (Chicago), and many others sprang into action to address the evolving needs of community members. (From "The Post-9/11 Backlash and Response," pp. 138, 140)

**Bullying in Schools**: According to the federal government, 28 percent of students in sixth through twelfth grade have experienced bullying. But the Sikh Coalition reported that up to two-thirds, or 67 percent, of Sikh American students report being bullied. The playground has always been a more fraught place in America for students of color, but in the week after September 11, the cloud of fear in the country engulfed South Asian, Muslim, and Arab American youth in new ways. (From "Bullying in Schools" inset, p. 149)

**Sureshbhai Patel**: On February 6, 2015, Sureshbhai Patel, a fifty-seven-year-old Hindu Indian man who was visiting his son in Madison, Alabama, was assaulted by local police officers in an apparent hate crime. Patel did not speak English, and a resident of his son's neighborhood had called the police on him for "suspicious" behavior, identifying Patel as a "skinny Black man wearing a toboggan." The police used excessive force, including slamming Patel to the ground, causing him to be paralyzed from the waist down. (From "Sureshbhai Patel" inset; p. 153)

**"Don't Play in the Sun!"**: Skin color is an integral part of the South Asian experience in the United States. During colonial rule, the British cemented the use of skin color to stratify South Asians. Now, popular culture and media (such as Bollywood) perpetuate the saliency of skin color. Dark skin tones have consistently been associated with negative or villainous traits. Advertisements for skin-bleaching creams are common and rarely contested. The persistent and systemic equating of dark skin to evil and of light skin to good within the South Asian community has resulted in darker skin being the marker of undesirability and inferiority (which is also linked to anti-Black attitudes). (From "Brown," 172–73)

**Forging Solidarity**: In August 2014, Michael Brown was shot and killed by a police officer in Ferguson, Missouri. The response to this murder made #BlackLivesMatter visible as a national movement. Many queer non-Black South Asians recognized that our fight for justice is intimately tied to Black liberation. Queer South Asians started and joined #APIs4BlackLives collectives, organized solidarity actions, raised money for the movement, and marched in the streets with Black friends, family, and communities. (From "Queer South Asians in America," p. 185)

## Activity 2: South Asian Women Workers

1. *Opening Discussion*: What words come to mind when you hear the word "nanny"?

2. Share the definition of a "domestic worker": "A person who works within an employer's household. Domestic workers perform a variety of household services for an individual or a family, including childcare or eldercare, cleaning, and housekeeping. Some domestic workers live in the house where they work."

3. Ask students what they know about domestic work, if they know a domestic worker (if their family employs one or someone in their family is a domestic worker), and what types of working conditions domestic workers face.

4. Read the section on Nahar Alam and domestic workers (pages 332–36) and this article on Andolan: Organizing South Asian Workers: bit.ly/andolanNYC ("How to Turn a Grueling, Thankless Job Into a Movement" for the *Nation*, by Michelle Chen, July 3, 2014).

5. Discuss what students learned from the materials.

6. If able to secure the film *Claiming Our Voice* (21 minutes), screen it and discuss. The film is available for purchase here: claimingourvoice.com. A companion curriculum to the film discussing domestic workers' rights and working conditions can be found here: bit.ly/COVcurriculum ("Screening Guide & Companion Curriculum for the Film 'Claiming Our Voice'" by Promiti Islam and Monisha Bajaj).

**Activity 3: Resisting Violence and Xenophobia**

1. Ask students to define the term "xenophobia." After a brainstorm, provide the definition "dislike of or prejudice against people who appear to be foreign or from other countries" and ask students if they have ever witnessed xenophobia before.

2. Have students watch these three short videos:

    - Opening sequence of *Divided We Fall*, at bit.ly/dividedfall (*Divided We Fall: Americans in the Aftermath*, directed and produced by Sharat Raju and Valarie Kaur, 2008). Full film available at valariekaur.com/film.

    - "What Is the Sikh Faith," at bit.ly/sikhfaith ("What Is the Sikh Faith: 'In America, We Can't Even Get Our Hate Straight,'" from CNN's *United Shades of America with W. Kamau Bell*).

    - Sikh rapper spreading his message, at bit.ly/mandeepsethi ("Meet the Sikh Spreading His Message through Rap," from CNN's *United Shades of America with W. Kamau Bell*).

3. Pass out this article on the Oak Creek Sikh temple shooting for students to read in small groups: bit.ly/oakcreekgurdwara ("Seven Killed in Wisconsin Sikh Temple Shooting," BBC, August 6, 2012).

4. Have students work in small groups to discuss how xenophobia relates to bullying and hate crimes. Ask students to also discuss ways to address xenophobia and hate. Have groups report back on ideas they came up with.

## Activity 4: Organizing for Change

1. Ask students what they understand by the term "collective action." Brainstorm and then provide this definition: "The behavior or actions of a group working toward a common goal. When individuals engage in collective action, the strength of the group's resources, knowledge and efforts is combined to reach a common goal shared by the entire group."

2. Make copies of the following sections of the book and distribute. Ask students to work in pairs to read their assigned section and take notes.

    - "The Parrot's Beak" (pp. 24–27)
    - "Ghadar Party" (pp. 36–40)
    - "The Civil Rights Movement" (pp. 85–88)
    - "DRUM and the NCSO" inset (p. 138)
    - "Eckshate" inset (p. 164)
    - "SALGA and the India Day Parade" inset (p. 186)
    - "Jahajee Sisters" (pp. 194–97)
    - "Hindu Temple Joins Sanctuary Movement" inset (p. 220)
    - "Organizing for Immigrant Rights in Los Angeles" (pp. 243–47)
    - "A Quiet Persistence: Turning Point for Women and Families" inset (p. 252)
    - "National Guestworker Alliance & Saket Soni" inset (p. 260)
    - "Nahar Alam" (pp. 332–36)
    - "Rights, Respect, and Recognition" (pp. 337–40)
    - "Bhairavi Desai and the New York Taxi Workers Alliance" inset (p. 350)

3. Have each pair report back to the class what they learned from the section and anything that surprised them or they would like to learn more about.

## Activity 5: Visual Timeline of South Asian American History

1. Make copies of selected images from *Our Stories*.

2. Using the timeline handout on pages 32–37 of this companion guide, cut out each historical entry. Shuffle the images and historical descriptions and place them around the room.

3. Ask students to arrange a timeline with the correct images and chronology of entries on the board or a wall of the classroom. This can also be done with a clothesline and clothespins to create a hanging timeline across the classroom.

4. Once complete, have students take turns reading the historical entries.

5. Discuss what students learned from the activity.

If possible, have students explore this interactive timeline of Asian American history ("A Different Asian American Timeline," produced by ChangeLab) in depth: aatimeline.com. This can be done in class or at home as homework. Have students journal and report back on what they learned from exploring the timeline.

# DISCUSSION PROMPTS FOR DEEP READING OF OUR STORIES

In the prompts below, educators are asked to have students read sections of *Our Stories* and engage with the following questions.

PROMPT 1

The vague term "South Asia" is defined in different ways by politicians, policy makers, historians, and geographers and also has a range of everyday meanings. Most definitions of "South Asia" include the modern-day countries of India, Pakistan, Bangladesh, Sri Lanka, Nepal, Bhutan, and Maldives. Afghanistan is often considered part of "South Asia," and some analysts also regard Myanmar as part of South Asia. Within and among these various countries are countless distinct ethnic groups, languages, religions, cultural milieus, political statuses, and historical traditions. The idea of "South Asian American" identity becomes even more complicated when we remember that people come to America not only directly from South Asia, but also as "double migrants" from South Asian diasporic populations created through histories of indentured labor. Thus, "South Asian Americans" might come from places such as Fiji, the Caribbean, or Africa.

1. After reading selections from *Our Stories: An Introduction to South Asian America*, you have been exposed to a few slices of South Asian American life. What other South Asian American groups/histories/stories would you like to learn more about, and why? What questions or concerns do you have about the way "our stories" are presented in these selections? If you identify as a South Asian American, what would you add to this collection, based on your South Asian American story?

PROMPT 2

In arguing before the U.S. Supreme Court that he should be eligible for citizenship, Bhagat Singh Thind declared that he should be considered white on the basis of his "high caste" status, and because of his birth in the northwest of India. To emphasize the purity of his purported whiteness, Thind reinforced a rhetoric of casteism, regional and religious bigotry, and anti-Black racism, proclaiming to the court that "the high-caste Hindu regards the aboriginal Indian mongoloid in the same manner as the American regards the Negro, from the matrimonial standpoint." Hence, if the Supreme Court had agreed that Thind was white and on this basis awarded him citizenship, it would not have followed that other South Asians would have been granted citizenship. In fact, a victory for Thind on the basis of his supposed racial distinctiveness might very well have strengthened the case *against* granting citizenship to other South Asians—notably South Asians from the northeastern and southern parts of the region, South Asians with dark skin, people from lower-caste backgrounds, Dalits, casteless people, people of "mixed" ethnicities, and non-Hindus. With this understanding, answer the following questions:

1. Thinking about the different South Asian individuals, families, and communities you have read about in *Our Stories*, name some people or groups who might have been harmed by a ruling in favor of Thind's argument, and explain why.

2. If you identify as South Asian, how would you respond to Thind's racial rhetoric, based on your own knowledge of your family's specific ethnic background, regional origin, caste assignment, perceived physical appearance, and/or religious tradition?

3. *Our Stories* includes numerous examples of South Asians who have worked in solidarity with Black activists and organizations to combat white supremacy, as well as South Asians who have been directly helped (sometimes in a lifesaving sense) through the interventions of Black activists and community members. Discuss some of these historical and contemporary figures. Imagine a conversation between one or more of these individuals and Thind—what do you think each side would say?

See the following sections for individuals to consider for this exercise:
- "Sick Keesar's Petition to Benjamin Franklin" (pp. 7–10)

# DISCUSSION PROMPTS FOR DEEP READING OF OUR STORIES

- "Lascar" inset (p. 9)
- "Histories of Racism in the United States" inset (p. 10)
- "Jumping Ship" (pp. 11–15)
- "Aladdin Ullah" inset (p. 13)
- "Visitors & Travelers" (pp. 16–23),
- "Bhagat Singh Thind" (pp. 52–57)
- "Changing Definitions of White" inset (p. 56)
- "The Civil Rights Movement" (pp. 85–88)
- "Dalit Panthers" inset (p. 87)
- "The 'Model Minority' Myth" inset (p. 112)
- "What Dr. B. R. Ambedkar Wrote to Dr. W. E. B. Du Bois" (pp. 177–81)
- "Black-Desi Secret History" inset (p. 178)
- "Responding to a Letter in the Chicago Defender" inset (p. 180)
- "Dalits and the Persistence of Caste" inset (p. 181)

## PROMPT 3

*Note: This prompt could be an alternative to Prompt 2, if students are not asked to read about Thind.*

As we can see from *Our Stories*, South Asians have at times been placed within the category of Blackness, and many South Asians have worked in solidarity with Black activists and organizations to combat white supremacy. At the same time, we also see that South Asians have often participated in and benefited from anti-Black racism. Given these complexities of racialization, resistance, and complicity, answer the following questions:

1. What are some historical examples of South Asians being racialized as Black? What does this say about racial categories themselves—e.g., Blackness, whiteness, Asianness?

2. Discuss some examples of interracial solidarity between people from Black and South Asian communities working together to oppose white supremacy. Name examples from different time periods. How

far back does this tradition of solidarity seem to extend, based on what you've read?

3. Discuss some examples of how South Asians have participated in and benefited from anti-Black racism. Have you personally observed or experienced racism in a South Asian community setting? Explain.

4. What is solidarity? What does it look like? Give examples.
    - Relationships forged through political struggle that seek to challenge forms of oppression.
    - Solidarity ≠ sameness
    - Solidarity = willingness to engage differences
    - Solidarity is fundamentally about an expanding love—one that goes beyond yourself, family, friends, and all those you know to those different from you, those you've yet to meet, and those you might never meet.
    - To make our "human condition count" it will take communities continuing to come together around common concerns, becoming tight-knit, and organizing collectively.

5. What kinds of things might allow space for solidarity, and what kinds of things might shut down the space for solidarity?

## Prompt 4

In the introduction to chapter 5 of *Our Stories*, Radha Modi notes that "often, stories of South Asian Americans are limited to their nationality, which results in narrow and homogenous depictions of the community." In opposition to this homogenizing idea of "nationality," Modi highlights the need to focus on *intersectionality*, or "the understanding that a person's life experiences encapsulate all their identities"—race, class, gender, sexuality, (non)citizenship, and dis/ability, among others. With this understanding, discuss the following:

1. Of the selections you've read from *Our Stories*, which ones do you think

particularly highlight the need for intersectional analysis, and why? [Suggested: Watch this video ("Kimberlé Crenshaw: What is Intersectionality?") of scholar Kimberlé Crenshaw on the definition of intersectionality: bit.ly/crenshawdefinition.

2. How does intersectional analysis call into question the idea of "South Asian America" itself? What are some examples of how another aspect of one's identity—being a refugee or a stateless person, for instance—can become more salient than an ethnicized or regional marker such as "South Asian" or "South Asian American"?

3. How does intersectional analysis help you better understand your own identity? Think about which aspects of your identity become more or less salient at different times, and how all these aspects of your identity shape and influence each other. Discuss.

## OVERARCHING DISCUSSION QUESTIONS FOR FURTHER EXPLORATION OF THEMES IN OUR STORIES

---

*These questions could also be useful for book clubs or study groups engaging with the book outside of a classroom context.*

1. How did South Asian Americans respond to acts of exclusion or acts of racial violence in the early twentieth century?

2. How have South Asian Americans participated in and benefited from anti-Black racism?

3. How were South Asian Americans inspired by other communities to organize and resist?

4. Whose voice/s do you find most compelling in these stories? What do you connect to or not connect to? How does geographical location, age, language, religion, sexuality, or gender identity shape how one constructs their South Asian American identity?

5. How has South Asian identity been constructed in relation to constructions of whiteness and Blackness, and how does that change over time? What are the ways in which South Asian identity intersects with other identities of color? In what ways do they not?

6. How is identity constructed? How is identity political? In this section of the book, what choices were made around identity and why?

7. Describe some of the political and social trends of the 1960s and 1970s that intersected with South Asian American activism on civil rights.

8. In the stories about post 9/11, how did racism impact South Asian Americans? What stories do you connect to, and why?

# DISCUSSION QUESTIONS BY CHAPTER

*The following questions can be used for general discussion or as "Essential Questions" for Lesson and Unit Planning. The distinction between "overarching" and "topical" follows the "Understanding by Design" framework for Unit Planning (Wiggins & McTighe, 2005).*

## Chapter 1: Early South Asian American History (pre-1923)

OVERARCHING

1. How did the migration patterns of South Asians relate to global economic and political shifts?

2. How did early South Asian Americans contribute to social reforms?

3. What is Orientalism, and how did it contribute to the experience of early South Asian Americans? How is it similar to and different from other types of racism? What is its relationship to anti-Black racism?

TOPICAL

1. How did early South Asian immigration patterns reflect the abolition of slavery and the resulting shift to low-wage and indentured labor?

2. How did early South Asians forge multiracial alliances (both personal and political) in the U.S.?

3. What obstacles (both personal and political) did early South Asian Americans encounter? What were some of their responses?

4. How did early South Asian Americans integrate anti-colonial resistance into their lives in the U.S.?

## Chapter 2: Forging Lives in Uncertain Times (1923–1965)

OVERARCHING

1. What impact does anti-Black racism have on immigrants of color?

2. How have immigrant groups attempted to integrate into "whiteness"?

3. What is scientific racism, and how has it been used to exclude or include immigrant groups?

4. How did immigration in this period reproduce, strengthen, or dilute differences of religion, class, and caste?

5. How are global activists connected to and informed by each other's struggles?

TOPICAL

1. How have South Asian Americans benefited from anti-Black racism and the caste system and also worked against these structures? How did they use these structures to attempt to "become white," and how were these structures used against them? What are some examples of this same dynamic, of benefiting from an oppressive structure while working against it, that you can see in the present?

2. How were South Asian culture, fashion, and yoga "Orientalized," or "exotified," in mid-twentieth-century American culture and entertainment?

3. How did South Asian political activism, including that of Gandhian nonviolent action, inform the U.S. Civil Rights movement? How did South Asians work in solidarity with African Americans?

4. How were South Asian political movements inspired by African American freedom struggles (for example, the Black Panther Party)?

## Chapter 3: Immigration after the Civil Rights Movement (1965–)

OVERARCHING

1. How do immigration laws help to create racial and class status in the U.S.?

2. What is the "model minority" myth? How might this myth contribute to the idea of "worthy" or "unworthy" racialized groups of people?

3. What are some ways that language is used to portray people as worthy or unworthy of inclusion in the U.S. (e.g., "illegal" vs. "undocumented," "chain migration" vs. "family reunification," "anchor babies," "model minority")?

TOPICAL

1. How did the 1965 Immigration Act help to create the myth of South Asians as a "model minority"? How does this myth simplify and obscure the backgrounds and experiences of South Asian Americans? How did family reunification, refugee resettlement programs, and the Diversity Immigrant Visa Program of 1990 help to diversify the South Asian American population?

2. What does the term "twice migrants" represent, and how are members of twice-migrant communities doubly impacted by coloniality, racism, and other forms of exclusion?

## Chapter 4: Post-9/11

OVERARCHING

1. What were the Third World Liberation Front strikes? How do they reflect Iyer's idea of a "more expansive vision of the United States"?

2. What is racial profiling, and how has it been used to surveil and control Black and Brown Americans?

3. What role did the state play in discrimination against South Asians after 9/11? How did processes such as special registration and detention reflect earlier moments of racist exclusion, such as Japanese incarceration?

TOPICAL

1. How did stereotypes of South Asian Americans shift after 9/11?

2. What were some community-based responses to post-9/11 racial violence, both by the state and by individuals?

**Chapter 5: Identity & Equality**

OVERARCHING

1. How do dominant narratives of minoritized communities contribute to the erasure of their experiences?

2. What is intersectionality, and how can it challenge dominant perceptions of what "identity" is and is not?

3. How can intersectional counterstories be used to challenge dominant narratives?

TOPICAL

1. What are some of the dominant narratives about South Asians in the U.S.?

2. How do the stories in this chapter expand or disrupt these narratives?

3. How do discrimination and exclusion appear in these counternarratives?

4. What role does colorism (or skin color discrimination) play in the South Asian American experience? How do South Asian Americans continue to resist these and other forms of oppression?

5. How did South Asians learn from and engage in solidarity with African American freedom struggles, both in the Civil Rights era of the 1950s and '60s and in today's anti-racist struggles?

6. How have queer South Asian Americans been marginalized and otherwise excluded from broader South Asian communities in the U.S.? How does this exclusion draw on colonial narratives? How do the people profiled in this chapter disrupt those narratives?

7. What role does the term "South Asian" play in disrupting these narratives?

## Chapter 6: Faith & Religion

Overarching

1. How do differences in religious practice reflect the diversity within an immigrant group, such as differences in geography, tradition, and personal choice?

2. What are some examples of religious communities acting as hubs for civic activism?

Topical

1. How have South Asian Americans asserted their right to religious practice in public spaces? What challenges and consequences have they faced? What have been some responses of the South Asian

community? How has their impact varied across different groups of the South Asian American diaspora?

2. How have South Asian religious spaces been contested or targeted?

3. How have South Asian Americans mobilized to create inclusion within religious spaces? How have these spaces been used in solidarity with other communities?

**Chapter 7: Civic Engagement**

OVERARCHING

1. How do the means, methods, and motivations for the political engagements of a community reflect its diversity?

2. How can communities participate in civic engagement beyond electoral politics? How does the availability of such spaces broaden who can participate?

3. What is intersectional organizing, and how can it help to examine and act on gender, class, and ethnic inequality within a community?

4. How did "guest work" become a form of indentured labor? What forms of indentured labor exist today, and how have South Asians organized against them?

TOPICAL

1. In the context of Islamophobia, xenophobia, and racial profiling, what are the dangers of perpetuating the trope of South Asian culture as uniformly oppressive and misogynistic?

2. What labor struggles have South Asians participated in? How have they organized across racial, economic, and international borders?

3. How have South Asian Americans used intersectional organizing to work against oppression, exclusion, and marginalization within their communities?

## Chapter 8: Arts & Popular Culture

OVERARCHING

1. How have sports, music, art, and fashion helped South Asian Americans to shape diasporic understandings of culture and ethnicity? How has participating in these cultural activities helped South Asians to connect within and outside of their own diaspora?

2. How do artists use their mediums to resist, complicate, and expand dominant narratives about ethnic communities?

3. What is the relationship between cultural arts and assimilation? How have cultural products (e.g., the Nehru jacket, Indian classical music) been used in this process? How can artists navigate the tensions around cultural commodification and appropriation?

4. How do new experiences help to shape and reshape an individual's relationship to their cultural identity?

5. How has South Asian American art and culture reflected evolving conceptions of identity, diaspora, and belonging, particularly across communities of color?

TOPICAL

1. How has "multicultural" literature evolved in the United States, and how is this reflected in South Asian American literature?
2. How have South Asian Americans used art to contest Orientalism, exotification, and other forms of "othering"?

3. How do the stories in this chapter reflect the influence of Black arts and culture on South Asian Americans? What are some historical conditions that made these cultural connections possible?

**Chapter 9: Work, Labor, and Entrepreneurship**

OVERARCHING

1. How do specific industries become "pathways" for immigrant work? What are the roles of immigration policy, family/social networks, and gendered work in constructing these pathways?

2. What is the relationship between the "model minority" myth and U.S. immigration policy?

3. How can labor organizing be a site for cross-racial solidarity? What lessons can we learn for continuing working-class solidarity in the United States?

4. Why is it important that labor organizing and other social justice work be led by those who are most directly impacted? What can people in positions of privilege do to engage in this work?

TOPICAL

1. How are caste and gender inequality reproduced in the work experiences of South Asian Americans?

2. How have caste and gender inequality informed the work of South Asian American activists?

3. How can South Asian solidarity be expanded across class lines? How can the workplace be a site for this solidarity work?

## Chapter 10: Family

OVERARCHING

1. Why is it important to illuminate underrepresented family histories?

2. What is the importance of "nontraditional" sites of kinship, such as social organizations (213), "chosen families" (394), community spaces, and activist spaces? How do these spaces help cultivate, bridge, and expand diasporic identities?

TOPICAL

1. How do the narratives in this chapter disrupt dominant narratives about South Asian American families?

2. What can the "First Days" stories in this chapter tell us about American culture? In what ways can new immigrants' perspectives provide insight into everyday American experience?

3. How do new and hybrid cultural traditions help to bridge South Asian American identities?

# HANDOUTS ON SOUTH ASIAN AMERICANS

## Who Are South Asian Americans?

According to Census data, nearly 5.4 million South Asians live in the United States. South Asian Americans trace their origins to **Afghanistan, Bangladesh, Bhutan, India, Nepal, Pakistan, Sri Lanka,** and **Maldives**. Some were born in these nations, while others are descended from immigrants from these nations. The community also includes double migrants—members of diasporic communities in the Caribbean (Guyana, Jamaica, Suriname, and Trinidad and Tobago), Africa (Kenya, South Africa, Tanzania, Uganda, Zanzibar), Canada, Europe, the Middle East, and the Pacific Rim (Fiji, Indonesia, Malaysia, and Singapore) who have subsequently migrated to the U.S.

The South Asian American community is diverse not just in terms of national origin, but also in terms of ethnicity, religion, and language. South Asian Americans practice the Baha'i Faith, Buddhism, Christianity, Hinduism, Jainism, Judaism, Islam, Sikhism, and Zoroastrianism; others have no faith. The most common languages spoken by South Asians in the United States, other than English, are Bengali, Gujarati, Hindi, Punjabi, Telugu, and Urdu.

South Asians are also diverse in terms of immigration and socioeconomic status. While some are citizens or permanent residents, others live here on short-term work visas, and others are undocumented. With respect to employment, there are notable concentrations of South Asians in the tech and healthcare industries, in education, and in service work, taxi work, domestic work, and the hotel and restaurant industry.

*Adapted from South Asian Americans Leading Together (SAALT)'s factsheets and from the curriculum "In the Face of Xenophobia: Lessons to Address Bullying of South Asian American Youth" (Monisha Bajaj, Ameena Ghaffar-Kucher & Karishma Desai, 2013), available online at bit.ly/xenophobiabullying.*

## Short Timeline of South Asian Americans in the U.S.

*Also see the excellent interactive timeline of Asian American history at aatimeline.com.*

### 1600s-1800s

Some South Asians were enslaved or indentured in the colonies that became the United States. For example, this ad by a slaveowner searching for a "runaway" "East-Indian" enslaved person in 1768 indicates the presence of enslaved South Asians in the United States.

*Courtesy of India Currents (bit.ly/indiacurrents).*

Mary Emmons, a servant or enslaved person of South Asian descent in the household of Aaron Burr (Founding Father and vice president of the U.S.), gave birth to two children fathered by Burr: (1) Louisa Charlotte, who married a free Black man and whose son Frank Webb Jr. became a novelist (publishing the second novel ever written by an African American, *The Garies and Their Friends*, in 1857); and (2) John Pierre Burr, who became a well-known abolitionist and who opened a barbershop that served as a stop on the Underground Railroad.

### 1838

By 1838, approximately twenty-five thousand Indian laborers have been transported as indentured workers to the British sugar colony of Mauritius. By 1917, more than 3.5 million South Asians will have been transported to European colonies in Africa, the Caribbean, and the Pacific as indentured "coolies," often undertaking harsh work once performed by enslaved people for a "penny a day," as historians have noted. *[Slavery was abolished throughout the British Empire in 1834 and will be abolished in the U.S. in 1865.]*

### 1880s & 1890s

Approximately two thousand South Asians are residing in the U.S. On the West Coast, many are farmworkers from the Punjab region who are members of the Sikh faith. Others are students. *[The modern nations of India, Bangladesh, Pakistan, Sri Lanka, and Burma were all part of the British Empire from the mid-nineteenth century to the late 1940s.]*

**1907–1908**
The Asiatic Exclusion League, an anti-Asian nativist group, opposes immigration from Asia and sparks violent race riots against South Asians in Washington, California, and Oregon in order to drive out "cheap labor." The Bureau of Immigration and Naturalization issues directives to dissuade citizenship applications from "Hindoos" (a derogatory term inaccurately applied to all South Asians; of the early migrants, 85 percent were Sikh, about 13 percent Muslim, and only 2 percent Hindus).

**1912–13**
Sikh migrants build the first gurdwara (Sikh temple) in the U.S. in Stockton, California, in 1912. A year later, founders of the gurdwara also found the Ghadar Party. Ghadar leaders galvanize a cross-class community of laborers and students to fight the British by connecting colonialism to the racist conditions of labor and life they are experiencing in the U.S. As the Ghadar Party expands, it establishes its official headquarters in San Francisco. Its leaders attract the attention of the British government, who recruit U.S. immigration officials to keep tabs on Indian nationalists in America, to limit the growing strength of Ghadar's revolutionary aims.

**1917**
The Immigration Act of 1917 defines a geographic "barred zone" in the Asia-Pacific (including South Asia) from which no immigrants can come to the U.S. *[World War I lasts from 1914 to 1918.]*

**1910s & 1920s**
State Alien Land Laws prohibit transfer of land to noncitizens and ownership by noncitizens; as a consequence, Indian farmers lose more than 120,000 acres in California. In the following years, more than three thousand South Asians return to their homelands due to xenophobic pressures. Migrants still come to the U.S. as traders or merchants through port cities such as New Orleans and New York, and some settle in African American and Puerto Rican communities. *[Women in the U.S. are granted the right to vote in 1920.]*

**1923**
In the *United States v. Bhagat Singh Thind* decision, the U.S. Supreme Court finds that South Asians are ineligible for U.S. citizenship because they are not white. *[In 1924,*

*U.S. president Calvin Coolidge signs the Snyder Act, giving Native Americans U.S. citizenship, but many states still denied them the right to vote until decades later.]*

**1946**
The Luce-Celler Act grants naturalization rights and small immigration quotas to Asian Indians and Filipinos, including a national quota of one hundred per year for immigrants from India. *[World War II lasts from 1939 to 1945.]*

**1957**
Dalip Singh Saund, a South Asian American from Imperial Valley, California, is elected to the U.S. House of Representatives in 1956 and serves from 1957 to 1963. South Asian Americans number more than twelve thousand. *[In 1955, the Montgomery bus boycott started in Alabama. In 1956, the Supreme Court declared segregation on buses to be unconstitutional.]*

**1965**
*The Immigration and Naturalization Act, which removes quotas for Asian immigrants, triggers the second wave of South Asian immigration. [In 1965, President Lyndon B. Johnson signs the Voting Rights Act.]*

**1966–77**
Eighty-three percent of South Asians enter the United States under employment visas, including twenty thousand scientists, forty thousand engineers, and twenty-five thousand medical doctors.

**1987**
In Hoboken, New Jersey, Navroze Mody is beaten to death by members of the Dotbusters—a violent hate group active in the state. South Asian Americans number more than two hundred thousand in the United States. *[The year 1989 marks the fall of the Berlin Wall and the beginning of the end of the Cold War.]*

**1990**
The third wave of South Asian immigrants begins, including H-1B visa holders (many working in high tech), students, and working-class families.

**2000**
Hamtramck, Michigan, is the first jurisdiction to provide language assistance in a South Asian language—Bengali—to voters, following a lawsuit by the Department of Justice.

**September 11–17, 2001**
Attacks against the World Trade

Center and the Pentagon take place on September 11, 2001. In the week following 9/11, there are 645 reports of bias incidents aimed at persons perceived to be of Middle Eastern or South Asian descent. South Asians Balbir Singh Sodhi of Arizona, Waqar Hasan of Texas, and Vasudev Patel of Texas are all killed in post-9/11 hate crimes. Harassment and threats make up more than two-thirds of all reported bias incidents.

**September 2001–February 2002**
The U.S. government detains, without charge, about 1,100 individuals, many from India and Pakistan. Many are denied access to counsel and undergo secret hearings. Many are detained for months on end; others are deported with no evidence ever presented of terrorist activity.

**2002**
The FBI reports that after 9/11, reports of violence against Muslims rose by 1,600 percent. Nineteen people are murdered in hate crimes prompted by the events of 9/11.

**2002**
The National Security Entry-Exit Registration System (NSEERS), or Special Registration program, requires non-citizen men and boys, ages sixteen and older, from twenty-five Asian and African countries (twenty-four of them predominantly Muslim, including Pakistan and Bangladesh) to report to their local immigration office for fingerprinting and interrogation. More than ninety-three thousand people register throughout the country over the course of the program's ten years. None are ever charged with any terrorist-related activity. More than thirteen thousand people are placed in deportation proceedings, while thousands more voluntarily leave the country.

**2005**
Piyush "Bobby" Jindal becomes the second South Asian American member of Congress. Many South Asians are elected to state office. *[In 2007, Jindal becomes the first-ever South Asian American state governor (Louisiana). Nikki Haley becomes the second in 2011 (South Carolina). Haley later becomes the U.S. ambassador to the United Nations under Donald Trump (2016).]*

**2012**
A white supremacist walks into a Sikh gurdwara in Oak Creek, Wisconsin, and opens fire, killing six and wounding four. The shooting is

labeled an act of "domestic terrorism."

**2010s**
According to the 2010 U.S. Census, there are 3.5 million people of South Asian descent in the United States. In 2012, Ami Bera from California becomes the third South Asian American to be elected to the U.S. House of Representatives.

**2015**
On February 6, Sureshbhai Patel, a fifty-seven--year-old Indian man who is visiting his son in Madison, Alabama, is assaulted by police officers in a residential neighborhood. A resident had called police to report "suspicious" behavior by a "skinny Black man" walking around the predominantly white neighborhood. The police use excessive force, slamming Patel to the ground, which is caught on the dashboard camera. Patel has to be hospitalized and is partially paralyzed as a result of the injuries. The police officer is at first fired due to international uproar, but then reinstated in 2016, and later acquitted of all charges.

**2016–19**
After the November 2016 election of Donald Trump, hate crimes skyrocket across the U.S. Islamophobia and xenophobia targeting anyone with brown skin result in many deaths and injuries. In February 2017, two men originally from India are chatting after work at a bar in Kansas. Asking them about their legal status and yelling at them to "get out of my country," a white man opens fire, killing Srinivas Kuchibhotla and wounding his friend Alok Madasani as well as Ian Grillot, who is at the bar and tries to help the men who are being attacked.

**2020/2021**
Kamala Devi Harris, a Black and South Asian senator from California, becomes the first woman of color nominated to a major party's ticket as vice president, to be elected (2020), and to be sworn in to the vice presidency of the United States (2021).

**2020s**
There are now nearly 5.4 million people in the United States who trace their heritage to South Asia. The dates in the timeline represent only a very small fraction of the names and histories that comprise the South Asian American community. As you continue learning about South Asian America, re-

member to seek out the voices that reflect the diversity of South Asian American experiences.

*Adapted from "South Asians in the U.S.: A Social Justice Timeline," developed by SAALT.*

## GLOSSARY OF TERMS

**Anti-Black racism**: Anti-Blackness or anti-Black racism is a term to highlight the ways in which Black people in particular experience racism. While many racial and ethnic groups experience racism or prejudice, the term anti-Black racism underscores the unique experiences of racism for Black people.

**Casteism**: Adherence to a caste system. In South Asia, caste is a system of religiously codified exclusion that has created entrenched structures of oppression. These structures have been carried to and reinforced in South Asian diasporic communities across the globe, including in the U.S.

**Collective action**: The united action of people working together and pooling resources to achieve a common goal.

**Dalit**: A term that can mean "broken," "scattered," or "downtrodden." It is used today by those formerly called "untouchables" (and the *adivasis*, or indigenous peoples of South Asia) under the caste system, a religiously codified system of oppression. The term may have first been used in relation to caste oppression by the nineteenth-century reformer Jotirao Phule, but it was popularized by the economist and Dalit leader Dr. B. R. Ambedkar in the 1930s, and revived in the 1970s by the radical Dalit Panthers.

**Dehumanization**: The process of depriving individuals or communities of their full humanity, dignity, and equal personhood. Dehumanization can take place in individual interactions, but it more often occurs in systemic mistreatment of particular communities based on their race, ethnicity, national origin, immigration status, sexual orientation or gender identity, religion, or other characteristics.

**Domestic worker**: A person who works within an employer's household. Domestic workers perform a variety of household services for an individual or a family, including childcare or eldercare, cleaning, and housekeeping. Some domestic workers live in the house where they work.

**Islamophobia**: Dislike of or prejudice against Islam or Muslims, or anyone perceived to be Muslim.

**"Model minority" myth**: The harmful idea that certain groups are so successful that they are able to transcend their social status as minorities. This cultural expectation is often placed on Asian Americans, including South Asians, and creates a false narrative that all Asians are smart, wealthy, and hardworking—which in turn is used to argue that Asians are less in need of government assistance and are more deserving of praise than other communities of color, thus dividing those communities and perpetuating anti-Black racism.

**Orientalism**: A way of seeing Middle Eastern and South, Southeast, and East Asian cultures that exaggerates and misrepresents differences between these cultures and those of Europe and the United States (or "the West"). The Palestinian author Edward W. Said, in his landmark book, Orientalism, emphasized the way that this biased view was used as a tool to affirm colonial rule and continues to be used to justify Western imperialism globally.

**Racism**: Prejudice, discrimination, or hatred directed against someone based on their race or perceived race. Structural racism refers to the formalization of a set of institutional, historical, cultural, and interpersonal practices within a society that benefits members of one racial or ethnic group over others.

**Solidarity**: Mutual support among individuals in, across, or between communities and groups who have common interests and goals.

**White supremacy**: The belief that people who identify as white are superior to other racial and ethnic groups and, as a result, should dominate society.

**Xenophobia**: Dislike of or prejudice toward foreigners or of anything that is or is perceived to be foreign, even if it is not.

## FURTHER RESOURCES

**Lessons and Curricula on South Asian Americans**

- Bajaj, Monisha, Karishma Desai, and Ameena Ghaffar-Kucher. *In the Face of Xenophobia: Lessons to Address Bullying of South Asian American Youth.* 2013. bit.ly/xenophobiabullying.

- Bajaj, Monisha. "Countering Islamophobia through Education." Learning for Justice, May 2, 2017. bit.ly/counteringislamophobia.

- Islam, Promiti, and Monisha Bajaj. *Screening Guide & Companion Curriculum for the Film "Claiming our Voice."* bit.ly/COVcurriculum.

- South Asian American Digital Archive Lesson Plan Collection: saada.org/in-the-classroom.

- Queer South Asian National Network. *It Starts at Home: Confronting Anti-Blackness in South Asian Communities.* December 19, 2014. bit.ly/qsann

**Online Digital Resources**

South Asian American Digital Archive: saada.org

Interactive Asian American Timeline: aatimeline.com

Black Desi Secret History: blackdesisecrethistory.org

Dalit History Month Timeline: bit.ly/dalithistorytimeline

Solidarity Stories: solidaritystories.org

## Films

*Claiming our Voice* (Jennifer Pritheeva Samuel, 2013, 21 mins.) bit.ly/claimingourvoice

*Divided We Fall* (Valarie Kaur and Sharat Raju, 2008, 90 mins.) valariekaur.com/film

*Oak Creek: In Memoriam* (Valarie Kaur, 2012, 9 mins.): bit.ly/oakcreekmemoriam

*Becoming American: The Journey of an Early Sikh Pioneer* (Sharat Raju, 2009, 11 mins.): bit.ly/sikhpioneer.

*Continuous Journey* (Ali Kazimi, 2004, 87 mins.) bit.ly/continuousjourney.
 - Excerpt from *Continuous Journey* on Democracy Now!: bit.ly/continuousexcerpt.

Asian Americans series (PBS, 2020, 5 hrs.): pbs.org/weta/asian-americans

Additional documentary films are listed at the SAADA website: saada.org/resources/documentaries

## Selected Further Reading

Bald, Vivek. *Bengali Harlem and the Lost Histories of South Asian America*. Cambridge: Harvard University Press, 2013.

Bald, Vivek, Miabi Chatterji, Sujani Reddy, and Manu Vimalaserry, eds. *The Sun Never Sets: South Asian Migrants in an Age of U.S. Power*. New York: NYU Press, 2013.

Dhingra, Pawan. *Life Behind the Lobby: Indian American Motel Owners and the American Dream*. Stanford: Stanford University Press, 2012.

Iyer, Deepa. *We Too Sing America: South Asian, Arab, Muslim, and Sikh Immigrants Shape Our Multiracial Future.* New York: The New Press, 2015.

Maira, Sunaina Marr. *The 9/11 Generation: Youth, Rights, and Solidarity in the War on Terror.* New York: NYU Press, 2016.

Mathew, Biju. *Taxi!: Cabs and Capitalism in New York City.* New York: The New Press, 2005.

Prashad, Vijay. *The Karma of Brown Folk.* Minneapolis: University of Minnesota Press, 2001.

Prashad, Vijay. *Uncle Swami: South Asians in America Today.* New York: The New Press, 2012.

Ramnath, Maia. *Haj to Utopia: How the Ghadar Movement Charted Global Radicalism and Attempted to Overthrow the British Empire.* Berkeley: University of California Press, 2011.

Sohi, Seema. *Echoes of Mutiny: Race, Surveillance, and Indian Anticolonialism in North America.* Oxford: Oxford University Press, 2014.

Made in the USA
Middletown, DE
28 March 2025